D0459877

The Basic Essentials of
CANOEING

by Cliff Jacobson

**Illustrations by
Cliff Moen**

ICS BOOKS, Inc.
Merrillville, Indiana

THE BASIC ESSENTIALS OF CANOEING

Copyright © 1988 by Cliff Jacobson

10 9 8 7 6

All rights reserved, including the right to reproduce this book or portions thereof in any form or by any means, electronic or mechanical, including photocopying, recording, or by any information in writing from the publisher. All inquiries should be addressed to ICS Books, Inc., 1 Tower Plaza, Merrillville, IN 46410.

Printed in U.S.A.

DEDICATION

To Harry Roberts, editor of *Canoesport* Magazine. Thanks Harry, for your encouragement and for publishing my first article in *Wilderness Camping* Magazine.

ACKNOWLEDGMENTS

A special thanks to my friend and publisher, Dr. Bill Forgey, who at the start, believed in the worth of this book. Appreciation should also be extended to my editor, Tom Todd, and to the following magazines for permission to reprint portions of my articles.

To Dave Harrison, editor of CANOE, for use of my material which appeared in: November 1980 *Canoe Buyer's Guide* (How to get what you want in a canoe). And also to Art Michaels, editor of *Boat Pennsylvania* and *Pennsylvania Angler* magazines for use of my articles which appeared in these issues: *Boat Pennsylvania*, Jan./Feb. 1987, March/April 1987; *Pennsylvania Angler:* July 1986.

Published by:
ICS Books, Inc.
One Tower Plaza
107 E. 89th Avenue
Merrillville, IN 46410

Library of Congress Cataloging-in-Publication Data

Jacobson, Cliff.
    Canoeing : the basic essentials.

    (Basic essentials series)
    Includes index.
    1. Canoes and canoeing. I. Title. II. Series.
GV783.J28 1988   797.1'22   87-36161
ISBN 0-934802-39-4

TABLE OF CONTENTS

1. HOW TO CHOOSE A CANOE
— A primer on modern canoe design —

Contrary to popular belief (and the claims of some manufacturers), there's no such thing as a "perfect" canoe — or even an "all around" canoe. No single watercraft, regardless of its design, materials, or quality of construction, can do everything well.

It's unrealistic to expect a single canoe to win flatwater races on Saturday, clean house in whitewater slalom on Sunday, and confidently truck the family and 150 pounds of camping gear on a three-week stint across wilderness waters. It's equally absurd to expect that same canoe to weigh in at 40 pounds and hang together when it's wrapped around a mid-stream boulder. Even if such a canoe existed, its high price would put it out of reach of even the most discriminating paddler. Canoes, like cars have distinct personalities — a major reason why serious canoeists often own several canoes.

Since I can't put you into the "perfect" canoe — or even the best one for your needs — I'll instead offer some guidelines to help you make intelligent buying decisions. In the process, I'll suggest some ways to keep you from getting ripped off when you plunk down your hard-earned dollars on a new or used boat. First, some terms and design principles to build on (Note that a complete glossary of canoe terms is found in Appendix A).

Length

Other things being equal, the longer the canoe, the faster it will be. Canoes are *displacement* hulls; their maximum speed (displacement speed), which says nothing about the effort required to reach that speed, is determined by the formula: S (speed) equals 1.55 times the square root of the waterline length. Simple math reveals that an 18½-foot canoe can be driven 6.7 miles per hour, while a 15-footer, 6.0 miles per hour. A small difference perhaps, but one which can translate into "ease of paddling."*

The displacement formula breaks down some in water that is less than three feet deep. That's because a hard pushed canoe produces a substantial bow wave which is difficult to climb over. The result is loss of speed. Racers refer to this phenomenon as "climbing" and combat its effects by paddling canoes with wide buoyant sterns. Hence, the development of the asymmetrical canoe — a grand performer in shallows, yet equally formidable in the deep.

Rule One: Other things being equal, the longer the canoe, the faster it will be. And if you want the best shallow water performance, opt for asymmetry below the waterline.

On a negative note, canoes which are very asymmetric are often fickle (unpredictable) in tricky currents. For this reason, you're best advised to avoid these craft for use on whitewater or on twisty, muscular rivers.

Stability and bottom shape

Canoes usually have either high *initial* stability (the boat feels steady when it sets flat on the water) and low *final* stability (resistance to capsizing), or vice versa. It's impossible to maximize both variables unless the craft has a very wide molded beam.

High initial stability is best typified by a hull which is very flat in cross-section (see Figure 1-2). High final stability is characteristic of a more rounded hull.

A flat bottom canoe at first feels stable, but when heeled past the bilge, turns turtle without warning. On the other hand, round or Vee bottom canoes (see Figure 1-2) feel shaky initially, but they

---

* Racers commonly exceed the maximum displacement speed of their canoes by planing them for short distances. Most of us, however, will never push our boats hard enough to plane them, so "displacement speeds" — and the ease it takes to reach them — are most meaningful.

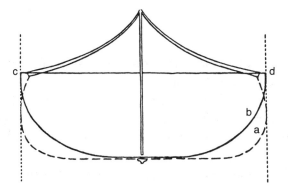

Figure 1-1. The inward curve of the sides of the canoe above the waterline, is called "tumblehome" (canoe "a"). Canoe "b" has flared sides, which are much more seaworthy. Note that the maximum beam (c-d) is the same for both canoes.

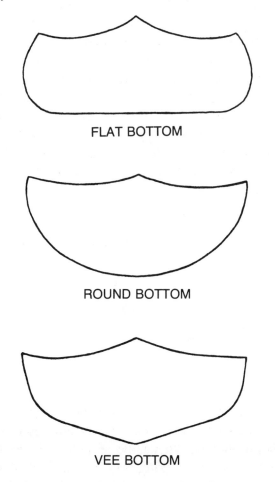

FLAT BOTTOM

ROUND BOTTOM

VEE BOTTOM

Figure 1-2. Flat bottom canoes have high initial stability and low *final* stability. Round and bottom vee canoes usually have the opposite.

firm up when heeled and thus resist capsizing. In short, rounded hulls are more predictable and controllable than flat ones on *all* types of water. And they're more easily propelled too!

Rule Two: Stability (initial and final), ease-of-paddling and seaworthiness is a function of hull shape. The round and Vee bottom hull excels in *every* category except initial stability. A canoe should have high final stability plus enough initial stability so you can paddle it without fear of capsizing. Unfortunately, most manufacturers boast the "initial stability" of their canoes, the less important of the two variables.

Keels

An external keel will make any canoe track (hold its course) better. However, it will also act as a cow-catcher in rapids; it'll hang up on rocks and cause upsets. There's smug satisfaction in watching your buddies spill when the keel of their canoe catches on the same rock that your "keel-less" canoe slid easily over just moments before. Later, when your friends have dried out you'll swear that your superiority in rapids is due to your impeccable paddling skill rather than a smooth bottom canoe.

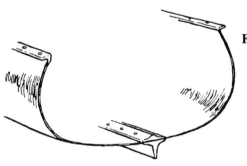

Figure 1-3. A standard or T-keel.

Let's not mince words. External keels are generally the sign of an inferior canoe design. A canoe which requires an after-thought tacked on below to make it paddle straight belongs back on the re-drawing board. Good tracking may be achieved simply by combining a round or Vee bottom, narrow ends, a straight keel line (more on this later) and somewhat squarish stems (ends). Aluminum canoes are formed in two halves, so they need a keel to hold the halves together. But even here, the keel could be mounted on the inside of the hull rather than the outside.

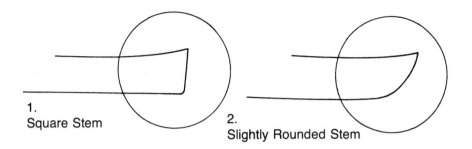

Figure 1-4. Canoe 1 has square stems; canoe 2 has rounded stems. Square stems promote straight-line tracking; rounded stems encourage turns.

The *real* reason for keels is to stiffen a floppy bottom. The biggest, flattest canoe bottom can be strengthened considerably by hanging a piece of angle aluminum or one-by-two along its length. Throw in a bunch of ribs and maybe a vertical strut or three — and the most shapeless hull will become rigid.

Figure 1-5. Canoes with shoe (whitewater) keels are more maneuverable and are less likely to catch on subsurface rocks than similar models with standard keels.

Rule Three: *Avoid canoes with keels. Exception — aluminum canoes which don't come any other way. Some aluminum canoe makers offer shallow draft "shoe" keels on their heavyweight white-water models. Shoe keels make a lot more sense than the standard T-grip rock grabbers (see Figure 1-5).*

Tumblehome

The inward curve of the sides of *some* canoes is called tumblehome (see Figure 1-1). It's used for two reasons: 1) Floppy materials like sheet aluminum need some curvature for strength. The alternative to tumblehome may be more ribs, hence more weight. 2) Tumblehome reduces the width of the canoe at the gunnels. Thus, you don't have to reach so far over the sides to paddle.

Tumblehome is used in varying degrees on some of the most sophisticated canoes. *But* when you wrap a tight bilge curve you sacrifice seaworthiness. A very skilled canoeist can bring a highly tumblehomed boat through some awesome pitches. The variable here is called SKILL — something too seldom mentioned nowadays. However, even experts agree that minimal tumblehome, or better some flare, is a much more seaworthy and predictable configuration.

Rule Four: *Avoid extreme tumblehome if you want a seaworthy canoe. Many flat-out race designs utilize excessive tumblehome for comfort of the paddlers; but these boats are not forgiving and should be avoided by all but highly skilled paddlers.*

Depth

Other things being equal, the deeper the canoe, the drier it will run in rough water. A center depth of around 12½ inches is plenty for a pleasure canoe, while an inch or two more is standard in wilderness trippers and whitewater craft.

Very shallow depth (less than 12 inches) is permissible in lightly loaded canoes that have seaworthy hull configurations (round or Vee bottoms with flared sides). Avoid high ends; they merely add weight and act as wind sails.

Beam

Beam is the distance across a boat at its widest point. As you can see from (Figure 1-1), "maximum beam" (c-d) may occur at the gunnels (gunnel beam) or someplace lower in the boat (waterline beam). Manufacturers' advertised *maximum* beam dimensions for canoes "a" and "b" would be identical, but the two boats would perform quite differently.

In an effort to provide more meaningful information about the paddling characteristics of their canoes, some manufacturers supply width figures at the 3-inch or 4-inch working waterlines. A narrow waterline usually means a fast, easy-paddling canoe. A wide water-line suggests the opposite.

Professional racing canoes are built to a formula which generally translates to a minimum beam of 27 inches at the 3-inch water-line; U.S. Canoe Association (USCA) competition cruisers follow the "4 and 32" rule — a 32-inch minimum beam at the 4-inch waterline.

It's probably okay for a wilderness tripping canoe to be wider at the 4-inch waterline than a USCA cruiser. An extra inch or two here might improve load capacity without noticeably affecting performance. On the other hand, it's doubtful you'd want a much beamier hull than a "4-and-32" for general cruising.

Rule Five: *If you want to race, buy a canoe built to the appropriate race class specifications. Otherwise, begin your search for the "ideal" hull with canoes whose mid-section measures within an inch or so of the "4-and-32" rule. Watch out for that old debbil tumblehome, and take a tape measure with you when you go shopping. Most canoe manufacturers print 4-inch waterline statistics in their catalogs.*

Figure 1-6. ROCKER: The fore and aft upward curve of the keel-line of a canoe is called "rocker." Rockered canoes turn more easily than those without rocker).

Rocker

The fore and aft upward curve of the keel-line of a canoe is called "rocker." A canoe with lots of rocker (anything over 1½ inches is a lot!) will turn easily in rapids and rise quickly to oncoming waves. But it will track poorly and be slower on the flats than a similar hull with no rocker.

Racers like a canoe with zero rocker — perhaps a hint of lift in the bow, but that's all. Whitewater canoes should have severe rocker — 3-inches is not uncommon. A wilderness tripper might fall somewhere in-between — about 1-1½ inches. The important thing to consider is *how* the boat will be used. A canoe that tracks like a mountain cat when near empty will turn with impudence when heavily loaded. A heavy load forces a canoe down into the water (acts like a keel) and so improves directional tracking. Wilderness canoes ordinarily are heavily loaded and therefore require some rocker. Conversely, it makes little sense to have lots of rocker in a minimally loaded day cruiser.

A canoe's length and hull configuration are important too. Short hulls need less rocker than long ones, and flat bottom canoes turn more easily than round bottom ones. Very short canoes — 14½ feet or less (solo boats) — with no rocker may be turned easily by leaning them on their side (you use the rocker in the sidewall). A rocker of more than one inch is ridiculous in a true solo canoe unless it's a flat-out whitewater boat.

Rule Six: *Use a tape measure to determine the amount of rocker in a canoe before you buy it. Simply measure the distance from the stem to the ground (note that asymmetric canoes usually don't have the same amount of rocker at each end). Figure on zero rocker for a racer, maybe a half-inch for a day cruiser, and up to 1½ inches for a wilderness tripper. For whitewater, the more rocker the merrier.*

Capacity

The advertised carrying capacity of a canoe is generally meaningless information. That's because about three-fourths of a canoe's load carrying ability is borne by the middle third of its length (Figure 1-7). Moreover, capacity figures tell you nothing about seaworthiness or how the canoe will perform when heavily loaded. In the example below, canoe #1 is much more seaworthy than #2 because its wide buoyant ends will rise over waves rather than knife through them. But #2 is definitely the faster of the canoes.

Rule Seven: *Advertised load capacities are generally meaningless. If you want a load carrier, select a hull with a profile similar to #1. If you want speed, choose a canoe with finer ends. Note that it's impossible to improve on both variables — speed and*

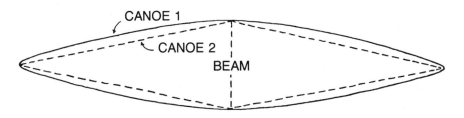

Figure 1-7. Capacity figures alone tell you nothing about how a canoe will perform when heavily loaded. Here, canoe 1 will handle a load much better than canoe 2 because its wide buoyant ends will rise over waves rather than knife dangerously through them. But canoe 2 is the faster of the two canoe types, all other things equal. Flaring the bows of canoe 2 — so they'll turn away waves — will significantly increase seaworthiness.

capacity — without changing the length of the canoe. That's why long canoes carry loads more effortlessly than short ones.

Weight and Strength

You can have a strong canoe or a light canoe, but it's unlikely you can have both unless you choose a very sophisticated and frightfully expensive ($1,200 plus) layup.

Look carefully at any 16-18 foot pleasure canoe which weighs less than 50 pounds. Most likely the strength isn't there, regardless of the manufacturer's claims. By the way, most canoe makers are "over-optimistic" in advertising the weights of their craft. Take your bathroom scale with you when you go canoe shopping and figure on a 5-15 percent "little white lie" factor.

Rule Eight: *You can have an ultralight and strong canoe only if you choose a very sophisticated and very expensive layup.*

Abrasion

Canoes generally die of abrasion, not from being wrapped around rocks. The harder the canoe's material, the better it will resist abrasion. Heat-treated aluminum ranks number one in the "drag it through the shallows" category, with Royalex ABS and Polyethylene not far behind. Epoxy-fiberglass is probably next, with polyester-fiberglass, wood-strip and wood-canvas finishing last.

Ease of Repair

If you use a canoe hard, you'll ultimately need to repair it. Canoes built of fiberglass and Kevlar are easiest to repair; a properly applied patch is hardly noticeable. Wood-strip canoes mend nicely, as do wood-canvas ones. It's possible to fix a Royalex ABS or aluminum canoe but the patch will be glaring reminder of the rock you hit. From an aesthetic viewpoint, polyethylene hulls cannot be repaired.

Despite what some canoe manufacturers say, no canoe-building material is "indestructible." So consider the merits of a less durable canoe that is easily patched over a more durable one that is not.*

Rule Nine: *No canoe is indestructible! Generally, the more durable the canoe material, the more difficult it will be to effect an invisible repair, and vice versa.*

Solo Canoe Considerations

The traditional requirements for length, depth and beam mentioned earlier don't apply to solo canoes. Most variables (speed, tracking, turning, portability, seaworthiness and general handiness) will be maximized in a canoe length of 14-16 feet; an outwale (outside edge of the gunnel) beam of 27-30 inches, and a center depth of 11-12 inches. Except for use in severe whitewater, additional depth is unnecessary since the paddler is located at the craft's fulcrum. It takes a very big rapid to bury the ends of even a low volume solo canoe.

Tumblehome is less of an evil in solo canoes than in tandem ones because a lone paddler doesn't need to coordinate his movements with a partner.

On Buying a Used Canoe

1.   Know the current retail price of the canoe before you buy it. Good canoes command around 80 percent of their current market value; cheapies 10 to 20 percent less.

2.   Stay away from the classified ads in newspapers unless you want a typical aluminum or polyethylene canoe. High-tech

---

* Detailed information on patching all types of canoes will be found in my book, *CANOEING WILD RIVERS*, ICS Books, Inc. 1984.

canoes are almost never advertised in newspapers. If brand names are not specified in the ad you can bet the canoe is junk.

3. Canoe races and paddling seminars are good places to frequent if you want a good buy on a used canoe. Canoe enthusiasts want their old "friends" to go to other enthusiasts, not to "canoers" who would rather fish than paddle.

4. Home-built canoes may be good or bad. The good ones are built on club forms and are advertised almost exclusively in canoe club newsletters and by word-of-mouth. The bad ones are usually constructed from plans supplied in popular magazines and are invariably advertised in newspapers.

5. Turn used canoes upside down and sight along the keel. Don't buy a canoe with a "hogged" (bent-in) keel. Once a keel or keel-line is bent, it's almost impossible to straighten properly.

6. Check fiberglass/Kevlar canoes for signs of hull delamination. A cloudy matrix tells the tale. Once delamination begins, it usually continues. Avoid these boats like the plague!

7. Don't over-react to minor surface damage: Galled varnish, scratched gel-coat and surface cracks in woodwork are easily repairable. But don't buy a canoe with a twisted stem, broken gunnel or hull that's out-of-round.

8. If a canoe looks out-of-round or twisted when you stand back a ways and view it, it probably is. Your eyes are a most accurate measuring device!

9. Good canoes *appreciate*. Bad ones do the opposite. You can't go wrong by buying a *good* used canoe.

2. HOW THEY'RE BUILT
— A lesson in fabrics, resins and materials —

Used to be you could choose from wood/canvas, aluminum and fiberglass canoes. Add lapstrake, plywood and wood-strip boats, and you defined the product line. In the early sixties, a few enterprising companies experimented with ABS plastic — same stuff used for football helmets — but the results were unsatisfactory. The ABS canoes cracked, split and literally came apart at the seams. By 1975, they had passed quietly into oblivion. No canoeist I know will mourn their passing.

Royalex
Around 1960, UniRoyal began to offer foam-cored ABS plastic to the canoe industry. And the Royalex canoe was born. It's been going strong ever since. Royalex is a thermoplastic laminate with an approximate half-inch thick blown plastic core. The number and thickness of laminations is specified by the canoe maker. Some Royalex lay-ups are quite substantial, others are merely adequate. You get what you pay for! An outer sheath of colored cross-linked vinyl protects the ABS from decomposing in the sun.

Royalex is extremely tough and slippery: It will slide over rocks that would stop aluminum canoes in their tracks and break or damage fiberglass or Kevlar craft. And Royalex has an excellent "memory": Wrap your canoe around a bridge piling and it'll probably pop back into shape with scarcely a crease.

Royalex can withstand severe impact but only limited abrasion. Continued dragging through shallows will reduce the smooth vinyl skin to a mass of deep cuts. Nonetheless, the product is incredibly durable — the favorite of whitewater daredevils.

Kevlar

In the early seventies, Dupont developed a honey-gold tire-cord fabric (now used widely in policemens' flak vests) they called *Kevlar*. Some world class whitewater paddlers built canoes and kayaks from the material and were so impressed by its strength, they nick-named it "holy cloth." Today, Kevlar is the staple fabric in every high performance canoe and kayak and is also widely used to reinforce selected areas of stock fiberglass canoes.

Kevlar is about 40 percent stronger than fiberglass and not quite half as light. It's very difficult to puncture or tear. Because Kevlar is so light and strong, many paddlers request boats built from "all-Kevlar" cloth. In truth, all-Kevlar canoes are not very durable; they frequently break from the inside. Unlike fiberglass, Kevlar cannot be sanded; it just frizzes up like cotton candy. Run a Kevlar hull persistently over sharp rocks and the bottom will look like it needs a haircut. Cosmetic repairs require real ingenuity. The solution is to cover the damaged "hair" with *fiberglass* cloth and resin then later sand to blend.

Composites of Kevlar and fiberglass are much more durable, easier to repair, and less expensive than the pure product. Many canoe makers are already building boats this way. Others may do so if you specify.

Fiberglass

Fiberglass technology has changed considerably in the last two decades. Where once the choice was between "chopper gun" and "hand lay-ups" (descriptions follow), there are now dozens (hundreds?) of proprietary lay-ups which utilize E-glass, S-glass, Kevlar, nylon, Dacron, carbon fiber and other materials in an array of dazzling configurations. Top-of-the-line hulls feature Hexcel (honeycomb) cores of Nomex, Airex, or PVC closed-cell foam for lightness and rigidity. Fiberglass simply isn't fiberglass anymore.

Before you can appreciate what's happening in fiberglass construction, you need to learn a few terms:

Fiberglass cloth is composed of twisted strands of fiberglass woven at right angles to one another. "Cloth" has the highest glass to resin ratio (about 1:1) of all the fiberglass materials, and also the greatest strength. The best fiberglass canoes are built of "all cloth" laminates.

Matt: Chopped crosslinked glass fibers held together with a dried resin binder. Matt has a glass to resin ratio of about 1:3, which means it's a third as strong as cloth. Matt absorbs a lot of resin and adds stiffness to a hull, so it's regularly used in canoe bilges where extreme rigidity is desirable. Matt is cheaper than cloth and it's much heavier. Most good canoes are stiffened with additional layers of cloth (more expensive) or roving, rather than matt.

Roving: Similar to cloth but with a coarser weave. Glass to resin ratio is slightly less than cloth but impact resistance is greater. Many of the best canoes utilize some roving as a stiffener.

E-glass and S-glass: E-glass is the common boat-building fabric which can be purchased at any marina. S-glass — a patterned material — is *much more* abrasion-resistant — and expensive! Some of the best whitewater canoes feature a layer of S-glass on the outside to better resist scrapes.

Gel-coat is an abrasion-resistant waterproof resin used on the outside of most fiberglass and Kevlar canoes. To save weight, some high performance canoes are built without gel-coat (called skin-coat construction). However, skin-coat craft are not a good choice for the recreational canoeist.

Canoe Building Resins

Polyester: Inexpensive, not very strong, and standard of the canoe-building industry.

Vinylester: Stronger, more flexible and only slightly more expensive than polyester. Most of the best Kevlar canoes are being built with Vinylester resins.

Epoxy: Strongest and most expensive of the boat building resins. Used by only a handful of custom canoe builders. Good boat building epoxies retail for 50 dollars or more per gallon, while polyester costs one-fourth as much.

Construction Lay-ups

Chopper gun: Chopped strands of fiberglass are mixed with polyester resin and sprayed into the mold. The resulting canoe is heavy, fragile and cheap. All the worst canoes are built this way. The tell-tale is the matrix of chopped fibers inside the hull.

Hand lay-up: Fiberglass cloth, and perhaps roving and matt, are laid into the mold by hand and saturated with resin then squeezed dry. You can see the cloth gridwork on the inside walls of the boat. A lot of very good fiberglass and Kevlar canoes are built this way.

Vacuum bagging: A plastic "vacuum bag" is placed into the mold and the air is pumped out. Originally, a vacuum cleaner was used as the power source, hence the name. The bag compresses the resin-soaked laminate and evenly distributes every ounce of resin so there are no pooled spots which add weight. This method produces the highest cloth to resin ratio possible. The very best canoes are built this way.

Pre-preg: Fiberglass (or more likely, Kevlar) cloth is pre-impregnated with resin then cured at high temperature in special (expensive!) molds. Pre-preg boats use miserly amounts of resin, so they are very light. Racing canoes built by this method commonly come in at under 25 pounds. On the negative side, pre-preg boats are very expensive and not very strong. Recreational paddlers should avoid them!

Color: Color adds weight to any fiberglass/Kevlar canoe. And generally, the darker the color, the greater the weight. That's because you have to add more color agent to the gel-coat to get a dark red color than a white one. The difference between white and red may amount to as much as five pounds in a typical 17 foot canoe. Be aware also that glass/Kevlar canoes scratch white (regardless of gel-coat color) when you hit rocks. For this reason, my favorite canoe color is white. It's also easy to get a good color match on a white canoe when repair time rolls around.

Foam Cores

A canoe bottom that flexes due to water pressure won't hold

its shape when paddled through the water. Ribs are traditionally used to stiffen a hull, but these exert unyielding stress on small areas which are subject to failure. Adding more material — cloth, roving, etc. — will also prevent "oil-canning," but it will also add weight.

For this reason, high performance fiberglass/Kevlar canoes are commonly constructed with an integral core of closed cell foam. The foam separates the laminates and produces an absolutely stiff wall — one which won't flex under pressure. There's a significant decrease in weight too, mainly due to the elimination of some layers of cloth. Foam-cored recreational canoes commonly weigh well under 50 pounds.

But all is not roses. A recreational canoe needs some flex so it won't destruct when it hits rocks. If the foam core doesn't break on impact, deep cuts which are cosmetically difficult to repair, often result. And replacing large areas of broken-out foam has been described as akin to "performing a lobotomy." In short, foam-cored canoes are ideal for racing and use on lazy waterways, but not for folks who will use them hard.

Let's summarize what we've learned about fiberglass/Kevlar construction:

1.   All-Kevlar canoes aren't as durable as those constructed from hybrid laminates. And they're much more expensive!

2.   Foam cores are ideal where light weight is the primary consideration. But cored boats are too rigid and difficult to repair for general use.

3.   Vinylester resin offers the best compromise between low cost and high strength/durability.

4.   A recreational canoe should have a gel-coat for abrasion protection. Skin-coat canoes won't take much abuse.

5.   Color adds weight to a canoe. White is the lightest color. You can specify a "clear" gel-coat (no color) to save weight but cosmetic repairs may be difficult later.

6.   Cheapest canoes are built with chopper-guns. Best are hand- laid or vacuum bagged. Pre-preg canoes are the lightest of their breed but they're not very durable.

Aluminum

Grumman brought out the first aluminum canoe just after World War II, and with few changes, the original 17-foot model is still in production. But Grumman hasn't remained idle: Their new *Eagle* defines most of what's new in aluminum technology. Built of 6010 alloy (25 percent stronger than traditional alloys), the 17-foot 66 pound *Eagle* features a gently rounded hull, relatively tall straight stems, and a full-flared (no tumblehome) shape that suggests it was designed by a naval architect. It was! The boat tracks straight, turns easily, and rides over monster waves without incident.

At this writing, 15, 17 and 18 foot aluminum canoes are available in traditional tumblehomed, buff-bowed designs from a number of manufacturers. If you like aluminum, look hard at 18-18½ footers which are by far the best paddling of the lot. *Demand* heat-treated aluminum, flush rivets or careful welding, and a minimal keel. Ultralight aluminum canoes (made of a thinner alloy) hold up well, even with rough treatment. Whitewater models which feature thicker hulls, shoe keels and extra ribs, should be your choice for running tough rivers.

If you occasionally apply a coat of paste wax to your canoe, you'll reduce its tendency to stick to rocks.

Polyethylene

The problem is academic: How do you stiffen bleach-jug material so it will hold the shape of a canoe hull? Coleman administered ribs, struts and an inner keel of tubular aluminum. This worked well enough to propel Coleman to the top of the canoe market.

Now, the furor has quieted. There's new technology in the wind. In 1984, Old Town discovered a unique way to stiffen polyethylene material. They sandwiched two layers of crosslinked polyethylene sheet between a three-eighths thickness of expanded polyethylene foam. The result was an incredibly rigid material which is as tough and forgiving as Royalex. The new canoe was named *Discovery* and it has revolutionized the canoe market.

Since there's no aluminum bracing in the *Discovery,* the craft can flex when it hits obstacles. Like Royalex, it can even be wrapped around a rock. Its "memory" returns it to shape.

Foam-cored polyethylene seems as strong and versatile as

Royalex and it weighs about the same. However, it's much less expensive.

Wood-Canvas Canoes

Wood-canvas canoes are not dead. They're just frightfully expensive! A limited demand exists for these traditional craft, which are hand built on a custom basis by a handful of small manufacturers. Enough has been written about these ancient but wonderful craft to delete further mention here.

Cedar Strip Canoes

Many of the canoes that win long-distance flat-water races are hand-built of cedar strips, nailed to a form, glued together and covered with fiberglass cloth and polyester or epoxy resin (the nails are removed prior to glassing). The resulting canoe is light, beautiful, and much stronger than most people think. As with all wooden boats, these canoes are expensive!

3. CANOE ACCESSORIES AND CONVENIENCES

If you're new to canoeing you may not realize just how much gear is required to outfit even a short float trip down a local stream. Besides the obvious — life jackets (PFD's) and paddles for everyone, you'll need cartop carriers, ropes for "tie-downs," a sponge and bailer, and "painters" (ropes for mooring the canoe), waterproof gear bags, first-aid kit and perhaps specialized items like carrying yoke and kneepads.

Fortunately, you don't need everything right now. All that's *absolutely* essential is a canoe, paddle and life vest, and some way to get it all to the river. Nonetheless, there are a number of low cost extras which will add measurably to your safety and fun. And these you'll want to get as soon as possible.

Here's what you *really* need:

Paddles

Given the choice between propelling a good canoe with a bad paddle or vice versa, I'd have to think on it. You just can't do good work with a shaved-down two by four!

Choosing a paddle according to your height has no rational basis because you *sit,* not stand in a canoe. Upper body length and the height of your canoe seat is the major factor in determining paddle length. If you want to be scientific about choosing a paddle:

1.   Set your canoe in the water and climb aboard.

2.   Measure the distance from your nose (height of the top grip) to the water. That's the *shaft* length. To this add the length of the blade (20-25 inches, depending on paddle style). That's the correct length for you. Note that the overall length of the paddle is in part programmed by the blade length.

If this procedure sounds like too much work, try these paddle lengths for starters: For typical aluminum and Royalex canoes — 56 to 60 inches. For high performance fiberglass/Kevlar cruisers — 52-55 inches.

Bent paddles: These have blades off-set 5-15 degrees (the 14 degree bend is most popular). "Bent-shafts" are *much* more efficient than straight paddles because their forward angled blades don't "lift" water (and waste power) at the end of the stroke. All effort goes into *forward* motion.

Bent-shafts are *the* choice for making time on flat water and for gentle cruising. Don't use 'em for whitewater though; they're too awkward.

The best paddles are constructed from carefully laminated woods and have tip protectors of lexan, polyurethane, stainless steel or Kevlar. You won't find good paddles in hardware stores or marinas!

Life Jackets (PFD's)

It should go without saying that anyone who canoes should wear a life vest. Always! "Canoeists" almost never break this rule. "Canoers" seldom follow it at all. A good PFD is the most important safety edge you can have. Buy a good one!

Avoid the orange horse collar styles which are bulky and uncomfortable to wear. Choose instead a zippered panel or ribbed vest filled with closed-cell foam. Try the jacket for fit as follows: Zipper and/or cinch the ties then grasp the vest by the shoulders and pull it up as high as you can. Does the jacket ride up over your ears? If so, keep shopping: It will perform likewise when you capsize.

Figure 3-1. Choose a zippered panel or ribbed foam-filled life vest.

Life jackets for kids: Proper sizing is even more important here as youngsters have little body fat (low buoyancy) and their weight is distributed differently than adults. Religiously follow the manufacturers sizing guidelines and *have the youngster try the jacket in a pool.* Absolutely never put an adult life vest on a small child! Drowning could result!

Don't compress life jackets when you store them or leave them in hot car trunks; the foam may harden and disintegrate.

Duct Tape
A roll of duct tape should accompany you on every canoe trip. Use it to fix everything from damaged canoes to holed tents. Duct tape is the canoeists gray badge of courage.

Nylon Ropes and Fabric-Covered Shock-Cord
Most essential is 100 feet of quarter-inch nylon rope. Cut the rope (singe raw ends with a lighter) into 15 foot lengths and coil each piece neatly. Four coils will do permanent duty as "tie-downs" for the canoe; two will serve admirably as bow and stern painters. Whatever is left will come in handy for something. You can never have too much rope on a canoe trip!

While you're poking about the hardware store, pick up a half-dozen steel S-hooks for use with your canoe tie-downs. Sharp bumper edges can slice the stoutest line, which is why you need S-hooks.

Figure 3-2. Shock-cord strung through holes in decks and thwarts provides security for your coiled painters and sundries.

Also buy about six feet of fabric-covered shock-cord. Thread lengths of shock-cord through holes in decks and thwarts (Figure 3-2) to provide security for your *coiled* painters and sundries. Ropes should *never* be left loose in a canoe where they can wind about your arms and legs in a capsize.

Waterproof Gear Bags
For casual float trips, any reasonably watertight container will do. Later, when you get serious about canoeing, you can consider the purchase of sophisticated packsacks and waterproof bags.

Inexpensive containers that are acceptably waterproof include plastic ice chests and ice-cream buckets (duct tape the lids shut to make them capsize proof), heavy-duty — four to six mil — plastic bags, and rubberized laundry bags. Plastic bags should be sandwiched *between* more durable nylon or canvas bags so they won't be punctured inside or out. An inexpensive burlap or polypropylene sack makes a good abrasion liner for the inside of a pack or duffel.

Security: Drill three-sixteenth inch diameter holes at six inch intervals along the inwales (inside gunnels) of your canoe and thread loops of parachute cord through the holes. When rough water threatens, *tie in your gear!* Use the chute cord loops to anchor your equipment tie-in's.

Yoke

You'll want a yoke even if your canoeing is limited to local waters with no real portages. Putting the canoe on and off your car, carrying it to the waterfront etc., often must be done alone.

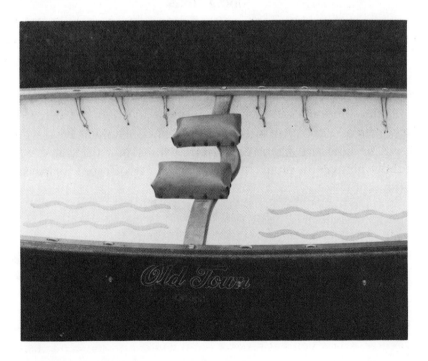

Figure 3-3. You'll want a yoke even if your canoeing is limited to local waters with no real portages.

At these times you'll wish you had a genuine yoke! Carrying even a light canoe on a pair of paddles tied between thwarts as recommended by some "experts" borders on insanity, even for those who relish pain.

The most comfortable set-up is a curved wood yoke with over-size (4½ inches by 8 inches) foam-padded shoulder blocks. Make your yoke from white ash and secure it to the gunnels with bolts.

Kneeling Pads

Necessary only if you're deadly serious about paddling whitewater. Cheapest (and best) pads are 12-inch squares cut from a closed-cell foam (ethyl-vinyl-acetate is the preferred foam) sleeping pad. Glue knee pads into the hull with *contact cement.*

Lining Holes

All canoes have some sort of hole or ring at each end for attachment of auto tie-down ropes and tracking lines. Ideally, ropes should be attached as close to the water-line of the canoe as possible to ensure good control when working the craft around obstacles in the river.

The solution is to drill a hole about three inches below the deck plate and epoxy in a length of half-inch diameter PVC waterpipe. The tube will keep water from leaking into the canoe when the bow plunges in rapids and provide plenty of room for passage of the rope.

4. CARRYING AND CARTOPPING YOUR CANOE

Every canoe trip includes some sort of portage — be it the task of loading the canoe onto the car, carrying it to and from the launching site, or lifting it over obstacles in a local stream. And if you're off to the wilds of Canada, portaging is part of the daily routine!

Contrary to popular belief, portaging is more an art than a feat of physical strength. I've seen 90 pound girls lift 75 pound canoes single-handed and carry them non-stop a quarter mile over very rough trails. And I've known 180 pound men who could not carry the same canoe more than 100 feet without dropping it on the nearest boulder!

Surprisingly, it's almost always easier to carry a canoe alone than with a friend. That's because partners can rarely coordinate their movements. Two person carries are only efficient on groomed trails, and then only when the canoe is outfitted with a yoke at *each* end.

Except in wind, a healthy adult can usually manage a canoe of reasonable weight without help if he or she has a good yoke and knows the correct "lift" procedures. The "Improved Side Lift" illustrated below is by far the easiest method.

25

Figure 4-1. One Person Lift: *Right* hand grasps yoke center and canoe is spun to thighs.

Figure 4-2. Step 2. *Left* hand grasps top gunwales forward of the yoke and canoe is balanced on thighs. Note location of right hand.

Procedure

1.   Roll the canoe on its side and grasp the yoke center with your RIGHT hand (Figure 4-1).

2.   The canoe is spun to thighs by lifting upwards on the yoke. As the canoe comes up, the left hand grasps the far gunnel *forward* of the yoke; right hand moves to near gunnel *behind* it. Nearly all the weight of the canoe is supported by your thighs (Figure 4-2).

3.   A forceful shove of your right knee and a snap of your arms brings the canoe to your shoulders. Simple as pie ... *If* you're quick about it! (Figure 4-3, 4)

Two person lift: If you want to conserve energy, try the "Two Person Lift." It's identical to the illustrated method except that your helper stands next to you *behind* the yoke, and you stand slightly in front of it. The canoe should be supported on the thighs of both you and your partner prior to raising it into position. Your hands will be forward of the yoke; your partner's will be behind it. Raise the canoe on signal together. Easy!

End lift: The end lift — where two partners lift the canoe by rolling it up on one end, should be avoided if you care about the cosmetics of your craft. Every time you "roll up," the grounded

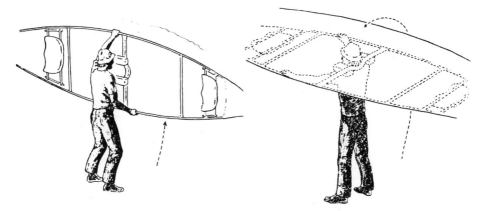

Figure 4-3. Step 3. With a quick upward push from your right knee, snap the canoe up and around over your head.

Figure 4-4. Step 4. Settle the yoke pads on your shoulders and ... relax!

end of the canoe (apex of the deck plate) takes a beating. Use this method on grass if you like, but avoid it on rocky ground and cement driveways.

Cartopping Your Canoe

Given enough rope, anyone can tie down a canoe so it won't blow off a car. The fun comes when you've got several boats to haul, or when the wind whips to impressive speeds. Here are the proven procedures for "event-free" cartopping.

Equipment: Get canoe racks that bolt directly to the car's drip eaves. Avoid models which put pressure on the roof. At this writing, one manufacturer (Yakima) offers a sophisticated carrier designed for use on cars with airplane style doors. And for "gutterless" trucks, there are always "Bronco brackets."

Canoe racks *must* be carpeted to prevent galling the canoe's gunnels. Racks which utilize one-inch tubular steel conduit may be sheathed in heater hose. Just lubricate the metal pipe with brake fluid and the hose will slide right on. Later, it will harden in place and make a neat looking unit.

Tie-downs: Each canoe should be tied down separately with two belly lines (tie lines as close as possible to the gunnels to prevent wind-shift) and *two* bumper lines at each end. Use S-hooks

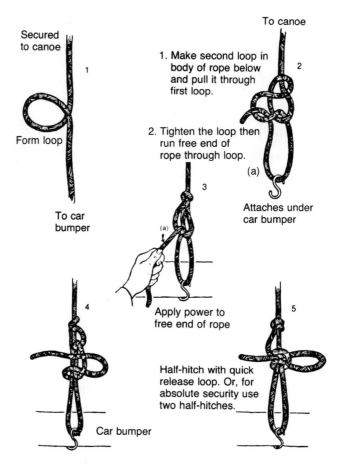

Figure 4-5. Power Cinch Sequence:

on raw bumper edges, or better, install eye bolts through bumpers for absolute security. Best hitch for tying down canoes is the "power-cinch" (Figure 4-5).

If you carry two canoes on one rack, tie a piece of carpet or boat cushion between them. This will prevent the hulls from contacting and damaging one another on a long drive.

You can carry a third canoe on a two car rack by setting it atop two 2 X 4's placed across the bellies of the canoes below. Tying down this mess requires securing the 2 X 4's to the cartop carriers. The view from the car will look like Charlotte's web and be as secure.

5. HOW TO PADDLE YOUR CANOE — THE BASIC STROKES

Somewhere among the pages of every elementary canoeing text you'll find these time-worn admonitions: Be *careful* when approaching rapids and falls; and don't paddle dangerous waters until you've had some *experience*.

Caution and *experience* — sound advice for a safe, event-free canoe trip. Don't you believe it.!

Some years ago, I helped rescue two canoeists who had inadvertently paddled over a 12-foot falls in Quetico Provincial Park, Ontario. They survived but their canoe didn't! It was a classic example of a canoeing accident which could have ended in disaster. Both men used *caution* when they approached the falls, and by their admission, were *experienced*. They just didn't know how to paddle! For a decade they had repeated the same errors with no bad effects. Then came the falls.

As the case illustrates, simply paddling a lot won't teach you the correct way to canoe. What will, is an understanding of the basic strokes and procedures.

Figure 5-1. Diagrams in this book will use this identification system.

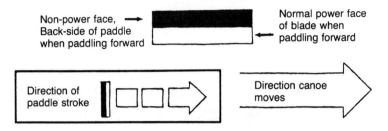

Non-power face, ➡
Back-side of paddle
when paddling forward

Normal power face
of blade when
⬅ paddling forward

Direction of
paddle stroke

Direction canoe
moves

Forward Stroke
(Used in both bow and stern)

Here's a stroke everyone "thinks" he knows. Just dip the blade in the water and pull back. Right? Almost. Fact is, the forward stroke is so sophisticated that canoe racers spend a good part of their lives attempting to perfect it. A few moments spent in a racing

Figure 5-2. Forward Stroke: Put your paddle in the water at least two feet in front of your body. Keep your top hand low — below your eyes.

START OF FORWARD STROKE

FINISH OF
FORWARD STROKE

canoe with a pro will instantly dispel any illusions of simplicity you may have about this stroke.

Begin the forward stroke as close to the canoe as possible and as far forward as you can without lunging. Keep your top hand low — *below your eyes,* and push! Most of the power is in your top hand; your bottom hand functions mostly as a guide.

Pivot your shoulders with the stroke so the paddle comes straight back, *parallel* to the keel. Don't follow the curve of the gunnel! When your lower hand reaches your hip, take the paddle out of the water and begin a new stroke. Bringing the paddle too far back wastes energy, and in fact, slows the canoe. This is because a paddle blade brought beyond vertical, pushes water *up,* which forces the canoe down into the water and slows its speed. This is why bent-shaft paddles — those with blades angled forward about 14 degrees — are more efficient than straight ones. At the end of the stroke, the angled blade points down. No water is raised, no speed is lost.

Return the paddle to its starting position by "feathering" (blade turned parallel to the water). This is especially important in wind.

The most common mistake beginners make is to paddle across their bodies. The paddle shaft *must* be perpendicular to the water, not at an angle to it.

Back Stroke
(Used in both bow and stern)

Most canoeists learn this stroke out of necessity when a rock looms ahead. It's one of the earliest strokes taught — and perfected — in whitewater canoeing.

Rotate your shoulders and begin the stroke as far back as you can. Use a levering action of your arms to pull the paddle through the water. Beginners will attempt to bring the paddle shaft across their bodies, which halves the energy of the stroke. The paddle shaft should be dead vertical.

Whitewater paddlers prefer an alternate form of this stroke which is nothing more than a "draw" (see following discussion) stroke applied parallel to the keel-line.

Procedure: Twist your shoulders a full 90 degrees towards your paddle side and look towards the stern of the canoe. "Draw" water forward, towards the bow. This "back draw" is extremely powerful and blends instantly into the conventional draw which is essential for correcting the ferry angle of a canoe in a strong current (see discussion in Chapter 6).

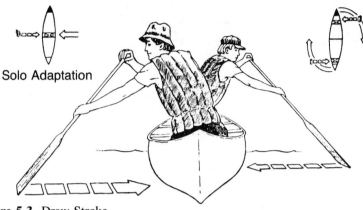

Solo Adaptation

Figure 5-3. Draw Stroke

Draw Stroke
(Used in bow or stern)

Old canoeing publications recommend the "bow rudder" for turning towards the paddle side. Now, this stroke has been replaced by the much more powerful and versatile "draw."

For maximum power and stability, execute the draw from a kneeling or well-braced sitting position. Reach as far out over the gunnel as you can, and power the paddle inward, forcing water *under* the canoe. When the paddle comes to within six inches of the hull, slice it out (backwards and up) and "draw" again. For maximum power, throw your body into the stroke.

The continuous power of the draw has a righting effect on the canoe which makes it almost impossible to capsize. However, once the power is released, you're at the mercy of gravity, so be sure your weight is well-centered in the canoe when the stroke is completed.

Cross Draw
(Used in bow of canoe only)

Basically an adaptation of the old "cross-bow rudder," it is nothing more than a draw stroke crossed over the bow of the canoe. Pivot at the waist, bring your paddle across the bow, reach far out … and "draw." The canoe will turn smartly towards the paddle side.

The cross draw is a solo or bow stroke only. It cannot be done in the stern of a tandem canoe. It is extremely powerful; when

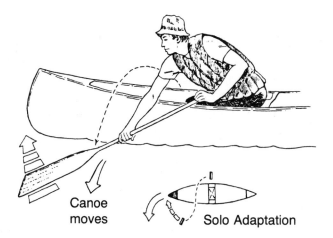

Canoe moves   Solo Adaptation

Figure 5-4. Cross Draw: A powerful stroke for turning to the off side.

coupled with a strong "stern pry," the canoe will literally pivot on its mid-point. The cross draw is also safe, as its shallow running blade cannot catch on rocks and upset the canoe.

Pry (Pryaway)
(Used in bow and stern of canoe)

The exact opposite of the draw. Begin the stroke under the bilge of the canoe and lever the paddle blade smartly outward, using the gunnel or bilge for leverage. Use an underwater recovery for this stroke. The mechanics of this will be obvious once you've tried it.

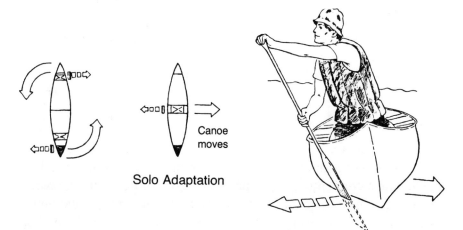

Canoe moves

Solo Adaptation

Figure 5-5. The Pryaway

Personally, I dislike the pry as it's very hard on paddle shafts and gunnels. Like the draw, however, the pry has a strong bracing action during the power phase. For this reason, it is preferred over the cross draw for turning the canoe in heavy rapids.

Warning: Don't use this stroke in shallow water. The paddle blade might catch on a rock and capsize the canoe!

J-Stroke
(Used in the stern only)

Beginners quickly learn that canoes don't paddle straight unless they are ruddered. A canoe moving forward veers away from the stern person's paddle side. Put her in reverse and the opposite applies.

The J-stroke is the traditional way to correct the problem. Begin the J as a typical forward stroke and finish with a gentle "kick" outwards (Figure 5-6).

START

FINISH

Thumb of top hand
is turned down.

Figure 5-6. The J-Stroke

There are a number of variations on the J. Some paddlers begin with a conventional forward stroke, but shortly after the blade enters the water, they start turning the thumb of the top hand down (away from their body) which changes the pitch of the blade. The amount of pitch is increased so that by stroke's end the blade is in a rudder position, thumb of top hand pointing straight down. If additional correction is necessary, a slight outward pry (J) will do the trick. The more pry, the greater the correction. This "pitched-J" or "Pitch" stroke is the most powerful and efficient of the various J-strokes.

Whitewater folk who scorn tradition and style, simply use a standard forward stroke and end it with a "thumbs up" stern pry.

When going backwards, the bow person has the most paddle leverage and so should use a "Reverse-J" to correct the course.

Minnesota Switch or "Hut" Stroke
(Used by both partners simultaneously)

The Minnesota Switch or Hut stroke was first used in the 1940's by Eugene Jensen and Tom Estes to win a series of canoe races. Instead of using the conventional J-stroke to maintain a straight course, Gene and Tom simply switched paddle sides on cue. Every 6-8 strokes, Tom would yell "Hut," and the two would trade sides. Over the years the stroke grew in popularity until today it is the preferred method for traveling fast. Virtually every competitive canoe racer uses it (with bent-shaft paddles, of course!), to the complete exclusion of the J.

The Minnesota Switch is very efficient — just what you need for trucking into the waves of a wind-tossed lake. But the canoe describes a somewhat erratic path through the water — the reason why traditionalists don't like it.

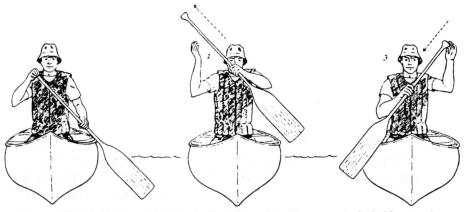

Figure 5-7. The Minnesota Switch: Switching sides is easy as 1, 2, 3. If correctly done only a split second is lost.

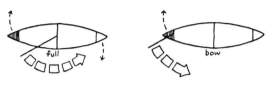

Figure 5-8. Full Sweep   **Figure 5-9.** Bow Sweep

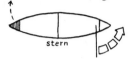

Figure 5-10. Stern Sweep: Canoe will accelerate and turn right.

Sweeps
(Bow or stern strokes)

Sweeps are useful in flatwater maneuvers for turning the canoe in a graceful arc. But compared to the powerful draws, crossdraws and prys, they are very inefficient. Nonetheless, they are part of the canoeing repertoire. The diagrams are self-explanatory.

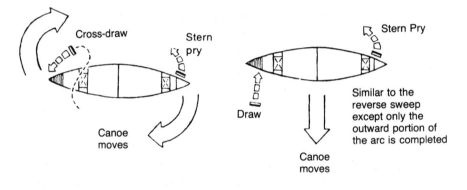

Figure 5-11a. The Pivot   **Figure 5-11b.** The Side Slip

Stern Pry
(Stern stroke only)

Similar to the reverse stern sweep except that only the outward portion of the arc is completed.

For greatest leverage, begin the stern pry as far back as possible. Thrust the blade outward with a snappy levering action of your arms, perhaps prying the paddle shaft off the gunnel or your thigh (if you're seated). Combine this stroke with a powerful crossdraw at the bow (Figure 5-11a), and the canoe will pivot on its midpoint. Use a "draw" at the bow instead (Figure 5-11b) and the canoe will slip sideways.

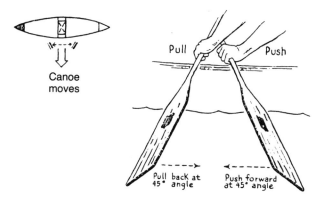

Figure 5-12. The Sculling Draw

Sculling Draw
(Useful in bow or stern of canoe)

The sculling draw is used to move a canoe sideways in water too shallow to effect a good draw. It's also a nice stroke in "heavy water" (powerful waves) as it has a strong bracing effect.

The sculling draw is hard to describe, easy to do and fascinating to watch. Perform this stroke in front of onlookers and you'll instantly achieve expert status.

Procedure: Place the paddle in the water a comfortable distance from the canoe, about two feet forward of your body. Rotate the leading edge of the paddle (normal power face of the blade) 45 degrees away from the canoe, and while maintaining this blade angle, pull the paddle backwards. At the end of the stroke, rotate the leading edge of the blade a full 90 degrees, and using the "same" power face of the blade, push water forward. The canoe will scoot toward your paddle.

The sculling draw is sometimes called the "Figure-8" stroke because the paddle describes this number as it is pulled through the water. That's inaccurate, however, as the path of the blade is nearly parallel to the keel-line of the canoe.

A "reverse" sculling draw will cause the canoe to move away from your paddle side.

Figure 5-13. The Low Brace

Low Brace
(Useful in both bow and stern)

The low brace functions as an outrigger to stabilize the canoe in turns and to keep it from capsizing in big waves.

Reach far out, paddle laid nearly flat on the water, palm of top hand up. Put your weight solidly on the paddle — a half-hearted effort isn't good enough. If you're capsizing, a powerful downward push will right you. The push should be fast and smooth.

The low brace is essential for turning into or out of eddies (see Chapter 6) and anytime you need to check a strong inside turn.

Figure 5-14. The High Brace

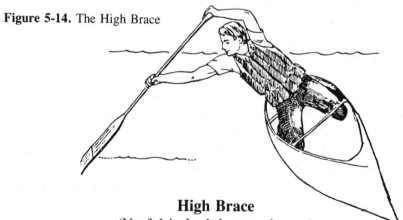

High Brace
(Useful in both bow and stern)

There are times when you need a strong brace, a draw, and a canoe lean all at once. Enter the "high brace." It's nothing more than a stationary draw with the power face of the paddle held against the current or at a strong climbing angle to it. Success depends on speed — either paddling or current — and a strong lean to offset the pull of the moving water. The high brace blends easily to the "draw" — an essential stroke for pulling into eddies and making sharp turns.

Figure 5-15. The Solo-C

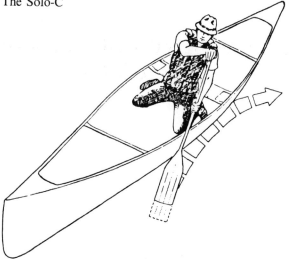

The Solo-C

This is the lone paddler's J-stroke; it's the only way to keep a canoe on course without adopting the Minnesota Switch.

Begin the stroke with a diagonally applied draw, then arc the paddle inward, *under* the canoe. Finish with a gentle outward thrust, not the powerful kick used in the J. Best results will be obtained if you progressively increase the pitch of the blade throughout the stroke. In the end, the thumb of the top hand should be turned straight down to facilitate this.

6. CANOEING IN WHITEWATER AND CURRENTS

We put ashore just above the drop then walked a well worn trail to the high rock outcrop which overlooked the rapid. Two college kids stood near the precipice effusively describing their plans to power around the big rock (Figure 6-1). I blotted out their mindless chatter and gathered my teen-age crew around me.

"Don't listen to those guys," I admonished quietly. "It's a piece of cake if you can ferry and a sure wipe out if you can't. Here's the plan: Soon as you clear the tree, kick the tail to the right and back paddle furiously. If the stern person is paddling on the left, a hard stern pry will bring the tail around. If the stern's paddling on the right, a draw at each end will do it. As soon as you've set the angle, back paddle — hard! You'll scoot sideways across the river into the clear channel at right. If you mess up and miss the ferry, you're done for!"

Any Questions?

While we were talking, the college boys shoved off into the current. Within seconds it was over. The inexperienced team broad-

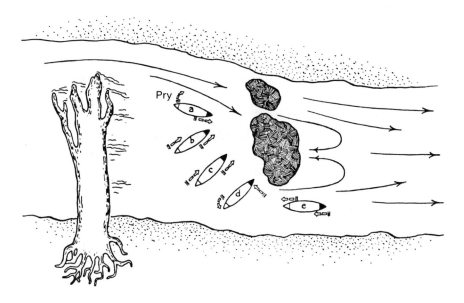

Figure 6-1. Back-Ferry To Safety (small arrows indicate direction of paddle movement).

sided the rock and capsized. Now, two men and piles of camping gear were in the frothy water. But there was no real danger; the pair floated safely to the quiet water below and were helped ashore by a half-dozen excited teen-agers.

When the way was clear, my crew began its descent. We coasted beyond the downed tree, ferried right, then scooted into the clear channel exactly as planned. It was a classic textbook maneuver and we earned grade A all the way.

I smugly congratulated myself for the two days of training I'd given this crew before the trip. But best of all was seeing the look of envy on the faces of those dripping wet young men when two 14-year old girls artfully negotiated the drop then did a perfect stern

first landing within yards of their still swamped canoe. There was
no denying that an ounce of skill outweighed a ton of macho!

Backferry, forward ferry, and in time, the eddy turn. These
are the techniques you must master if you plan to negotiate complex
currents. As the example illustrates, you cannot overpower a river.
But with the right skills, you can outfox it. Here's how!

Learn to Ferry!

Ferrying across currents is nothing new. Even the ancient
Egyptians were experienced in the art. They simply set the nose of
their barge at about 30 degrees to the current and powered ahead.
The two vectors — forward speed of the boat plus sidewash of the
current, carried them sideways across the river.

Whether you nose forward (the forward ferry — Figure 6-2)
into currents or backferry instead, depends upon circumstances. In

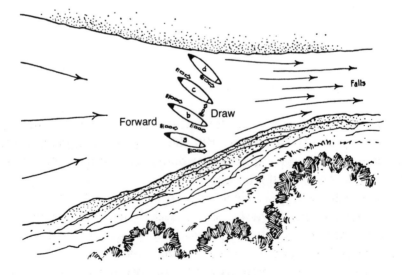

Figure 6-2. Crossing a River Using a Forward Ferry (arrows indicate direction
of paddle movement).

tight quarters, where quick turns are impossible, the backferry is preferred; for crossing large expanses of open water, the head on approach is recommended. Ferrying is a game of skill, not brute power. Here are the rules for safe passage:

1. First master the strokes outlined in the previous chapter. It's pointless to practice ferry maneuvers with your craft until you've learned to control the engines.

2. A ferry angle of around 30 degrees to the current is recommended. Less than this wastes energy, while more is difficult to maintain. There is a trigonometric relationship between the efficiency of the ferry angle and the downstream slip. In strong currents, it may be necessary to angle a full 90 degrees to the river's flow to get to the other bank with a minimum of downstream slide. *However,* 45 degrees is about the maximum angle-of-attack that most canoeists can hold. Since the penalty for "losing your angle" in a tough current is broadsiding — and possibly capsizing, you'll want to maintain a cautious approach. I usually test strong currents with a 15-20 degree angle. As confidence builds, I widen the angle, adding or subtracting as the need arises. Figure 6-2 shows the relationship.

3. Watch the shore when you ferry across large expanses of water. It's very difficult to maintain the correct angle without referencing your progress to a land marker of some sort.

4. The canoe must be trimmed dead level or slightly lighter at the *upstream* end. It requires a very strong team to back ferry a tail heavy canoe!

5. When ferrying forward, the stern has more paddle leverage than the bow. When backferrying, the opposite is true. This means that the *downstream* paddler has the greatest responsibility for correcting the ferry angle.

Once you learn to perform competent ferries, you'll discover all sorts of applications for the technique. Here are a few ...

Landing in Currents

Rivers run fastest at the center and slowest near the banks, so if you attempt to land nose first, the current will grab your tail and spin it downstream. In slow currents, the result is an uncontrolled eddy turn (Figure 6-5 shows a "controlled" eddy turn) — the mark of a novice. On a fast river, it's a neck-snapping spin and a possible capsize!

For these reasons, it's almost always best to *backferry* to shore. Simply tuck your tail in the direction you want to go, then paddle backwards. The harder you paddle, the more speed you'll scrub off. Ultimately, your stern will slide into the quiet water near shore and your bow will follow suit. Easy as pie and guaranteed to elicit admiration from your friends.

Negotiating Bends

Rivers flow fastest on the outside bends, the reason why novice canoeists are often swept tail first into them. So if you want to maintain control of your canoe in a tight curve, you'll have to backferry around it. Figure 6-3 shows the procedure.

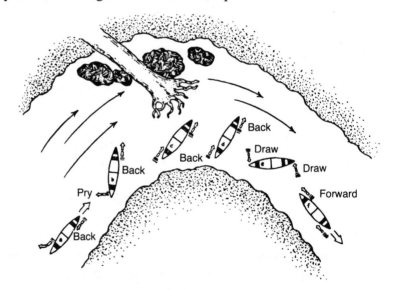

Figure 6-3. Ferrying Around a Sharp Bend: Keep away from the outside of the bends, except in low water (arrows indicate direction of the paddle movement).

Parallel Side-Slip

In very slow currents where a ferry is overkill, a simple side-slip maneuver may often do the trick. Strokes? Bow person draws while his partner prys, or vice versa (see Figure 6-4).

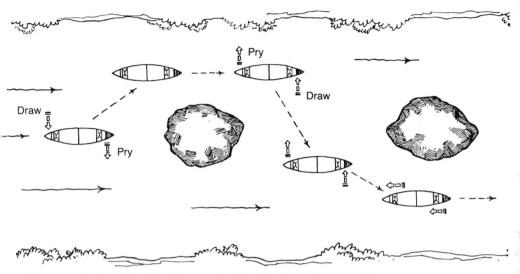

Figure 6-4. The Side-Slip: You can't side slip the average cruising canoe very fast, so use this maneuver for short distances only.

You'll quickly learn that you can't side-slip the average cruising canoe very far very fast, so rely on this maneuver for short distances only. A few inches of left or right side-slip is often enough to get you safely around a dead-ahead rock. Ferry and side-slip tactics are your best bet for avoiding the obstacles in a river.

Eddies Are a Safe Resting Place

Whenever water flows around a rock (but not over it!) a gentle upstream current or "eddy" is formed. Paddling long stretches of rapids can be nerve-wracking: The quiet water of an eddy is a convenient place to rest and collect your thoughts.

Since the movement of water within an eddy is opposite to that of the river's flow, there is a current differential at the eddy's edge. This is the "eddy line", and crossing it in strong currents can capsize you if you're not prepared for the consequences. If you cautiously poke your bow into the slow upstream current, the main flow of the river will catch your stern and spin it quickly downstream — as if a rug were pulled from beneath you. The result is a possible swim!

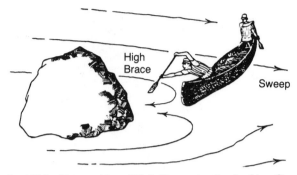

Figure 6-5. An Eddy Turn with a High-Brace in the Inside: Canoe must be leaned *upstream* when the bow crosses the eddy line

There are two ways to enter an eddy: By backferrying (the safest procedure), and by doing an "eddy turn" (the preferred method, once you learn the skills).

In Figure 6-5, the bow person "hangs on" to the calm water of the eddy with a high brace and lean, while the stern — who has not yet crossed the eddy line — also leans right to offset the centrifugal force. As soon as the turn is completed (takes a split second), the pair paddles up to the rock.

If, however, the partners were paddling on opposite sides, the roles — but not the canoe lean — would be reversed. Figure 6-6 shows the relationship.

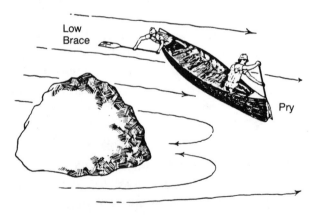

Figure 6-6. An Eddy Turn with a Low Brace on the Inside: Bow person may use a pry, as illustrated (preferred), or a crossdraw to turn the canoe into the eddy.

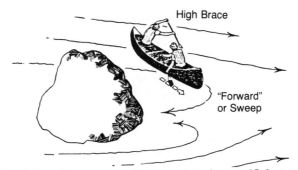

Figure 6-7. The Peel-Out: Canoe enters the current at about a 45 degree angle. Bow paddler uses a high brace and leans the canoe downstream as the bow crosses the eddy line.

Leaving an eddy (the "peel-out") is simple enough if you remember to lean downstream. In Figure 6-7 the canoe is angled at least 45 degrees to the current (a steeper angle than is used for backferrying) and power is applied. As the bow crosses the eddy line, the bow person high braces and leans downstream. The stern supports the lean and "sweeps" the canoe around. Figure 6-8 shows the procedure when paddle sides are reversed.

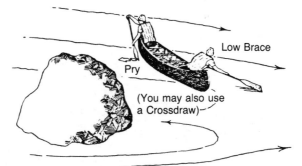

Figure 6-8. The Peel-Out: Using a low brace on the downstream side, the bow paddler stabilizes the canoe with a pry (illustrated) or a crossdraw as the current spins it downstream.

What about leaving an eddy by paddling out the weak lower end? In weak currents, that's possible; in big rapids the upstream current may be too powerful to overcome. Besides, small rocks often accumulate below large ones, which may prevent your leaving the eddy at the bottom end. Learn the eddy turn. It's an essential part of river canoeing!

Haystacks

When the fast water racing through a chute reaches the calmer water below, its energy dissipates in the form of nearly erect standing waves called "haystacks." A series of uniform haystacks indicates deep water and safe canoeing — that is, if they're not so large as to swamp the canoe. To help the bow lift over large haystacks, slow the canoe's speed by backpaddling, or quarter into waves at a slight angle. You can also lighten the ends (you should lighten *both* ends, not just the bow! by moving the paddlers closer amidships. If haystacks are very big, paddle the "edges" to keep from being swamped.

Choosing a Safe Course Through Rapids

Negotiating a complex rapid without incident requires skill, cool determination, an accurate appraisal of the dangers and a good partner. Here are the tenets of survival:

1.   An upstream vee indicates the location of rocks (Figure 6-9); a downstream vee is the safe approach.

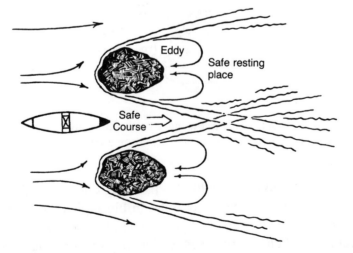

Figure 6-9. Choose a safe "downstream vee" when entering a rapid.

2. You can't steer around obstacles in a fast-moving river: Rely instead on the ferry techniques and side-slip maneuvers explained in the last chapter.

3. Scout rapids from shore before you run them, and view everything from a downstream vantage point. Often, a substantial ledge which is invisible from above, will be immediately apparent from below.

4. Proceed downstream *slowly* — backpaddle to reduce speed. Maintain control with effective draws, prys, crossdraws and ferry techniques.

5. Take advantage of eddies to recover your strength and plan your strategy for the water ahead.

7. HAZARDS

Canoeing in a Rough Sea

Running downwind: Running downwind on the crest of high waves is exhilarating but not always safe. The danger comes when the sea takes control and you begin to surf. Fortunately, canoes don't surf very well for very long. Invariably, the wave — and the scary ride it produces — will quickly pass. It's when a rocky shoreline looms ahead that you need to act fast. First, pour on the coal, which in itself is often enough to set you free. Failing this, bring the canoe to full speed then turn snappily into the wave (broadside it!). Brace hard on your paddles as the boat comes around, and *lean downwind!* Don't be surprised if you take a few gallons of water aboard.

A very good team can sometimes backpaddle off the wave without "losing it". Try this with uncertain skills, however, and you'll capsize for sure!

Some authorities suggest you lighten the stern in a following sea to prevent waves from swamping the canoe at the tail. In truth, if you simply maintain forward speed (keep paddling!), you'll usually have no trouble. You absolutely must maintain momentum or you'll lose control!

If water splashes in astern you must lighten *both* ends of the canoe by moving paddlers together, closer amidships. Lightening just the stern isn't good enough: Canoes don't run well with their bows (or sterns!) dragging. And they're not very controllable either.

Going upwind: Paddling upwind is *much* safer than going with the flow. To keep the bow from burying in big waves, lighten *both* ends. Paddle *straight into the waves:* Don't quarter them at an angle as recommended in most canoeing texts. Fact is, it requires an experienced team and a straight-keeled canoe to maintain a quartering angle in a rough sea. The penalty for broaching is a capsize! Use a fabric splash cover if you plan to canoe in heavy waves.

Loading for rough water travel: Canoes should be loaded *dead level.* Period! The only exception is for racing when proper trim may require a *slightly* heavy bow to overcome the canoe's tendency to "climb". Canoes will weathervane with the wind, so some experts advise you to trim the windward end down, which makes paddling easier. However, burying the windward end may allow water to splash in, producing a wet ride. And as I've said, canoes don't handle well with one end dragging!

My advice? Keep everything on the level and use proper paddling technique to control your canoe in wind.

Paddling alone is one time when you may wish to rearrange the load or change positions in your canoe. Just remember that canoes will weathervane, and move forward or aft accordingly. Figure 7-1 shows the relationship. Be aware, however, that the farther you get from the center of the craft, the less control you'll enjoy. Best practice is to assume a central position in the canoe and rely on good paddling technique.

Never canoe alone from a position on the stern seat: It's akin to paddling a seven foot canoe with a ten foot overhang. The slightest puff of wind and over you'll go!

Soloists should *always* occupy a position within two feet of the geometric center of the canoe. In calm water, it's okay to sit on the *front seat,* facing backwards.

Sweepers (also called "Strainers")
A sweeper is a downed tree which wholly or partially blocks

WIND DIRECTION

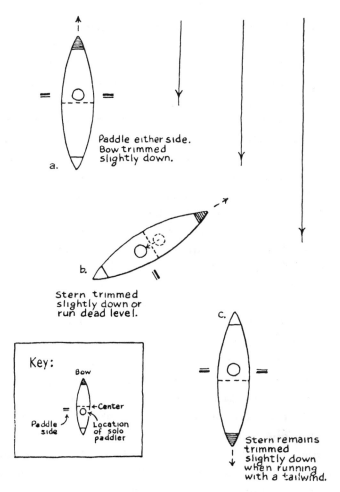

Figure 7-1. Paddling alone is one time when you may wish to rearrange the load or change positions in your canoe.

the flow of a river. It's one of the most dangerous of all river obstacles because its submerged branches can trap and hold a capsized swimmer or canoe. Even a very gentle current is strong enough to pin the most powerful swimmer in the branches.

Be particularly wary of sweepers which block outside curves, as the river's current will tend to force your canoe into them. If you capsize going into one of these brush piles and are trapped in the debris, escape — and rescue — may prove impossible!

The key to surviving an encounter with a sweeper is to avoid it! Hence, the importance of the *backferry*. If, despite your efforts, your canoe is carried into the branches of a fallen tree, keep calm, *lean downstream, and don't grab anything until the canoe comes to a complete stop.* At this point, worrying over the canoe is futile. Save yourself (if you can) by climbing onto the tree trunk.

If you capsize and are sucked into the branches, try to go through head first so you can clear a path with your hands. Under these conditions, any loose-fitting clothing (including your life jacket) may get snared by branches and keep you from surfacing. So shed what you can, if you can!

Most of the spring drownings on rivers are the results of encounters with fallen trees. Learn to backferry around bends and you'll have no trouble with these obstacles.

Hypothermia

Hypothermia is a medical term which means "low body temperature." It's usually the result of capsizing in cold water or of paddling in an icy rain without proper clothing. Symptoms begin innocently enough, first with pronounced shivering (not a reliable indicator, since some people lack the shivering reflex), followed by slurred speech and amnesia as the temperature drops.

At about 90 degrees Fahrenheit, shivering stops, muscles stiffen and the skin becomes blue and puffy. Unconsciousness and erratic heartbeat follow. When the temperature drops below about 78 degrees Fahrenheit, death results.

The table shows the approximate time the body can remain functional in cold water:

WATER TEMPERATURE	AMOUNT OF TIME BODY WILL REMAIN FUNCTIONAL
less than 40 degrees F.	less than 10 minutes
40-59 degrees F.	15-20 minutes
50-60 degrees F.	15-40 minutes
60 degrees F. and above	one or more hours

Numbers don't tell the whole story, however, as the shock of hitting cold water in a canoe upset may cause a heart attack — the reason why you need to wear a neoprene wet suit or waterproof outfit when you canoe frigid waters.

Treatment for hypothermia: Insulate the victim from the cold, wet environment. Replace wet clothing with dry, and administer *gentle, controlled* heat. Recommended procedure is to sandwich the stripped victim between two individuals of normal body temperature. Use a sleeping bag if you have one or pile on all the clothing you can find. You may administer warm drinks (no stimulants like coffee or alcohol) *only* if the victim can sit up and swallow.

Radiant heat from a fire is probably the quickest way to warm a victim of immersion hypothermia. However, radiant heat should be applied slowly and evenly. Excess temperature in a localized area may cause burns, as hypothermics have very little sense of feeling in their extremities. Treat the victim gently: Rough-housing may cause heart fibrillation and death.

Hypothermia is emotionally and physically draining. Plan to camp for a full day after the experience to allow the victim to recuperate.

Dams and Falls

Low falls can be run if there's a strong enough flow and the drop is not so steep as to produce a "hydraulic jump" (heavy backroller) at their base. If, after checking a falls, you decide it's safe to run, pick the point of strongest water flow and proceed at river speed over the ledge. As you reach the base of the falls, dig your paddles hard and deep to climb out of the trough below.

It's unsafe to run *any* dam, unless, of course, part of it has broken away. The danger lies in the well-formed backroller at the base, which is essentially an eddy set on edge. These backrollers are "keepers": They'll trap your canoe and recirculate it with the eddy flow. Escape means diving deep below the eddy line to the main flow of the river, where you'll be jettisoned out — a technique which requires a cool head and in-depth knowledge of what is going on.

I know several people who've survived encounters with dams. All agree it was the most frightening experience of their lives. Their advice? "Don't run any dam. Ever!"

Figure 7-2. It's unsafe to run any dam! The danger lies in the well-formed backroller which will trap your canoe and recirculate it with the eddy flow.

Self-Rescue

Everyone wants to be a hero and rescue someone. Fact is, in most canoeing accidents, you'll be rescuing yourself! Here are the suggested procedures:

Capsizing in rapids: Do not attempt to stand in water that is more than knee deep! A foot may become wedged between rocks and held there while the river mows you down. "Entrapment" is a major cause of drowning on fast moving rivers!

Immediately upon capsizing, get to the upstream end of the canoe. Hold tight to the stern and *keep your feet high,* away from the river's bottom. Try to swim the boat to shore using a modified backferry technique. Stay with the canoe unless doing so will endanger your life.

If you're thrown clear of the canoe and are forced to swim, immediately get on your back, *feet held high* to prevent somersaulting in the current. Your life jacket will keep you afloat. Use your feet and paddle to fend off rocks which might otherwise take their toll on your body. Swim ashore by backstroking (backferrying).

The canoe grounds on a partially submerged rock: As the canoe runs up on the obstacle, the current will rapidly whip the stern end downstream. Act fast! *Lean downstream* and brace with your paddle until the canoe comes to a dead stop. If the craft spins 180 degrees, it will probably slide off the rock if the bow paddler shifts his/her weight downstream.

If the craft broadsides against the obstacle, follow this procedure: Keep the downstream lean! One partner should brace on the downstream side while the other attempts to work the canoe free. If the rock is large enough, the nonbracing partner should step out on it and free the canoe.

If the rock is submerged, under the canoe's center, maintain the downstream lean as you shift weight around to free the canoe. if the water is shallow (less than two feet deep), get out on the *upstream* side of the canoe and push off. **Don't** do this in deep water: The current will suck you right under the boat!

In summary:

1. *Always* maintain a downstream lean and brace when you ground on a midstream obstacle.

2. Get out on the upstream side of the canoe only if the water is shallow.

3. Get out on the downstream side of the canoe only if you can climb up on the rock.

Canoe Over Canoe Rescue

If a canoe capsizes on reasonably calm water, you can perform a *canoe over canoe rescue*. Figure 7-3 shows the procedure. If you try the rescue in a current, be sure the rescue canoe is *upstream and perpendicular* to the swamped boat. As a final precaution, keep the "swimmers" upstream of the rescue boat, in the event the outfit plows into a rock. Here's the sequence:

1. The "swimmers" work their way to the rescue canoe and stow their paddles inside it. Together, the four paddlers position the swamped canoe perpendicular to the rescue boat. The rescue team rolls the swamped canoe on edge to break the air seal. Then they lift the bow of the canoe up onto the near gunnel. If necessary, the "swimmers" push down on the stern end of the capsized canoe to help raise the bow.

2. The swamped canoe is drawn, hand-over-hand across the gunnels, and the water is drained. Meanwhile, those in the water hold tight to the rescue boat.

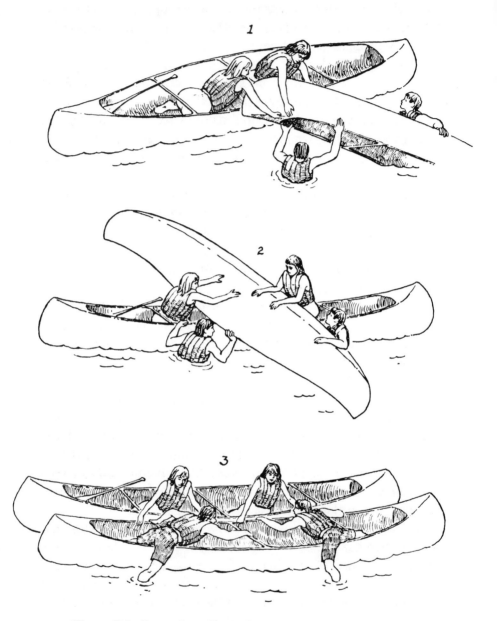

Figure 7-3. Canoe-Over-Canoe Rescue:

3.   The rescue team turns the canoe right-side-up and slides it back into the water. They then steady the craft while the "upset paddlers" climb aboard.

The entire process takes about three minutes.

Lightning

The often quoted advice to "get off the water" when lightning strikes, is sound. Unfortunately, this may not be possible if the shoreline is too unforgiving to permit a landing, or there is heavy pounding surf.

Nonetheless, a lone canoe on open water is ripe for an electrical strike, so if you can't put ashore, take these precautions: There is a cone of protection which extends about 45 degrees from the top of the tallest trees/land masses. Stay within this cone of protection but not so close that lightning could jump from the shore to you. Lightning can easily breach two dozen feet, so stay a few canoe lengths off shore as you work your way down the lake.

Since tree roots may act as electrical conduit, be wary of large trees near the water's edge. Roots spread more horizontally than vertically, which increases the size of the danger zone.

There's a notion that canoes built of wood or fiberglass are safer than aluminum ones in an electrical storm. No way! In fact, the opposite may be true. Ships are occasionally struck by lightning, usually with no ill effects. That's because the electrical discharge passes from the ship's antenna and/or lightning rods, around the hull and into the water. The metal skin of aluminum canoes may react similarly, providing your mass is below the gunnels (lay down in the boat!). Wood or fiberglass canoes may simply "fry."

All this is speculation, you understand. Best advice? Get to shore ... fast!

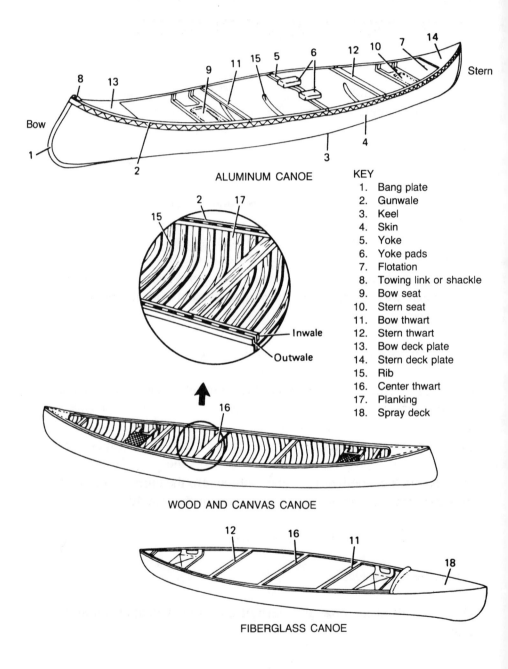

Bow

ALUMINUM CANOE

Stern

Inwale

Outwale

WOOD AND CANVAS CANOE

FIBERGLASS CANOE

KEY
1.   Bang plate
2.   Gunwale
3.   Keel
4.   Skin
5.   Yoke
6.   Yoke pads
7.   Flotation
8.   Towing link or shackle
9.   Bow seat
10. Stern seat
11. Bow thwart
12. Stern thwart
13. Bow deck plate
14. Stern deck plate
15. Rib
16. Center thwart
17. Planking
18. Spray deck

GLOSSARY OF CANOEING TERMS

Amidships: The center or middle of the canoe.

Bailer: A scoop (usually made from an empty bleach jug by cutting off the bottom) for dipping accumulated water from the bottom of the canoe.

Beam: The widest part of the canoe.

Bilge: The point of greatest curvature between the bottom and side of a canoe.

Bow: The front end of the canoe.

Broadside: A canoe which is perpendicular to the current of a river, thus exposing its broad side to obstacles in the water.

Broach: To turn suddenly into the wind.

Carry: See "portage."

Deck: Panels at the bow and stern of the canoe which attach to the gunnels.

Depth: The distance from the top of the gunnels to the bottom of the canoe when measured at the beam (sometimes called "center depth," as opposed to the depth at the extreme ends of the canoe).

Draft: The amount of water a canoe draws.

Flat water: Water without rapids, such as a lake or slow-moving river.

Flotation: Buoyant material set into the ends (or other places) of a canoe to make it float if upset.

Footbrace: A wood or metal bar against which a paddler braces his feet. Footbraces help secure the paddler in the canoe and so add to the efficiency of his strokes.

Freeboard: The distance from the water line to the top of the gunnels at their lowest point.

Gunnels (or gunwales): The upper rails of a canoe.

Hogged: A canoe with a bent-in keel or keel line.

Inwale: The inside portion of the gunnel.

Keel: A strip of wood or aluminum which runs along the center bottom of the canoe.

Leeward: A sheltered place out of the wind. Also, the direction *toward* which the wind is blowing.

Line: Rope used to tie up a canoe or pull it around obstacles in the water. Also refers to working a canoe downstream around obstacles in the water with the aid of ropes (lines) attached to the bow and stern.

Outwale: The outer portion of the gunnel.

Painters: Lines attached to the bow and stern of a canoe.

Planking: Lightweight boards nailed to the ribs on wood-canvas canoes. Its main purpose is to support the canvas.

Portage: The physical act of carrying the canoe over land.

Ribs: Lateral supports which run at right angles to the keel on the inside of a canoe. Ribs provide hull rigidity and structural strength.

Rocker: The upward curve of the keel line of a canoe.

Skid plate: A piece of thick Kevlar that is glued to the bottom ends of a canoe. Prevents abrasion of the skin of the canoe.

Splash cover: A fitted cover designed to keep water out of a canoe. Splash covers are useful in rough rapids and big waves.

Thwart: A cross-brace which runs from gunnel to gunnel.

Tracking: working a canoe upstream, against the current, with the aid of ropes (lines) attached to the bow and stern.

Trim: The difference in the draft at the bow from that at the stern of a canoe. A properly trimmed canoe will sit dead level in the water.

Tumblehome: The inward curve of the sides of a canoe above the waterline.

Water line: The place to which water comes on the hull of the canoe when it is set in the water.

White water: Foamy (air-filled) turbulent water.

Yoke: A special crossbar equipped with shoulder pads for portaging the canoe.

American Whitewater Affiliation International River Rating Scale

Note: This nationally recognized scale is used by whitewater canoeists to rate the difficulty of rapids. These ratings appear in many quidebooks and should be taken seriously. It's important to realize, however, that ratings change as water levels rise or fall. A rapid that rates Class I in mid-summer may be a dangerous IV during the spring run-off. So plan your trips accordingly!

Water Class and Characteristics

I. EASY — Easy bends, small rapids with low waves. Obstacles like fallen trees and bridge pilings. River speed less than hard back-paddling speed.

II. MEDIUM — Fairly frequent but unobstructed rapids with regular waves and low ledges. River speed occasionally exceeding hard back-paddling speed.

III. DIFFICULT — Small falls; large, regular waves covering boat. Expert maneuvering required. Course not always easily recognizable. Current speed usually less than fast forward-paddling speed. (Fabric splash cover useful.)

IV. VERY DIFFICULT — High, powerful waves and difficult eddies. Abrupt bends and difficult broken water. Powerful and precise maneuvering mandatory. Splash cover essential!

V. EXCEEDINGLY DIFFICULT — Very fast eddies, violent current, steep drops.

VI. LIMIT OF NAVIGABILITY — Navigable only at select water conditions by teams of experts in covered canoes. Cannot be attempted without risk of life.

APPENDIX 3

MAIL ORDER SOURCES OF QUALITY EQUIPMENT

Note: The companies listed below are those with which I've personally done business. Quality of equipment and service is first-rate!

L.L. Bean, Inc.
Freeport, Maine 04033
    An uncommonly nice company which still does business in the old world tradition. L.L. Bean is your best source of outdoor wear and footgear. The famous "Maine Hunting Shoe" is the most popular field boot in the world. Free catalog.

Recreational Equipment, Inc.
1525 11th Ave.
Seattle, Washington 98122
    REI is a co-op. You pay a few dollars to join and you receive a yearly dividend (about ten percent) on your purchases. The co-op specializes in mountaineering/backpacking equipment but also has a wide selection of outdoor clothing and general camping items.

Cabela's Inc.
P.O. Box 199
812 Thirteenth Ave.
Sidney, Nebraska 69162
    A wide variety (and quality) of equipment. Good prices, fast service. Extraordinary buys are sometimes possible.

Indiana Camp Supply, Inc.
P.O. Box 211, 1001 Lillian Street
Hobart, Indiana 46342
    Best source of medical supplies (they specialize in hard-to-get items for the medical emergency) and freeze-dried foods. Good selection of high-tech and traditional camping items. Overnight delivery — fastest in the trade.

Campmor
810 Route 17 North
P.O. Box 997
Paramus, New Jersey 07653-0997
    An incredibly complete catalog of outdoor gear. Everything from packs and tents to fabrics for repair are included. Good service, low prices.

Forestry Suppliers, Inc.
205 West Rankin St.
Jackson, Mississippi 39204

Your most complete source of forestry and surveying equipment — map aids, clear plastic for covering maps, compasses, etc. Also, lots of good knives, saws, and axes. Traditional camping equipment, too.

Cooke Custom Sewing
1544 Osborne Rd. N.E.
Fridley, Minnesota 55432

Outstanding pile and fleece outerwear, internal frame and soft packs, custom fabric spray covers for canoes, and hard-to-get specialty items for winter camping. Cooke Custom Sewing sews from their own proven patterns. Highly usable outdoor gear — no yuppie stuff. Also, custom sewing to your specs.

Martensen Company, Inc.
P.O. Box 261
Williamsburg, Virginia 23185

Liquid waterproofing material for maps.

Duluth Tent & Awning, Inc.
P.O. Box 16024
1610 W. Superior St.
Duluth, Minnesota 55816-0024

Your most complete source of canvas products, including Duluth packs for canoeing and traditional canvas camping and hunting tents. Duluth Tent & Awning will repair or customize tents and tarps.

Fast Bucksaw Co.
110 East 5th St.
Hastings, Minnesota 55033

Makers of what is, in my opinion, the best folding saw made.

Sierra West
6 East Yanonali St.
Santa Barbara, California 93101

A variety of well made clothing items. Sierra West has one of the best open-cell foam sleeping pads around.

The Ski Hut
P.O. Box 309
1615 University Ave.
Berkeley, California 94701

The Ski Hut manufacturers Trailwise equipment, made famous by Colin Fletcher in his book, *The Complete Walker*. They carry superb down-filled sleeping bags and outerwear as well as a good selection of general camping products. Ski Hut is known for its exquisite tailoring and fine workmanship on sleeping bags and parkas.

INDEX